RISE & SHINE
DAILY AFFIRMATIONS
FOR WOMEN

For general information on our other products and services or to obtain technical support, please contact our Customer Care Department within the United States at (866) 744-2665, or outside the United States at (510) 253-0500.

Rockridge Press publishes its books in a variety of electronic and print formats. Some content that appears in print may not be available in electronic books, and vice versa.

Cover Designer: Gabe Nansen
Art Producer: Sara Feinstein
Editor: Eun H. Jeong
Production Editor: Ellina Litmanovich
Production Manager: Michael Kay

Illustration used under license from Catherine Wheel Textures/Creative Market

Paperback ISBN: 978-1-638-07367-3
eBook ISBN: 978-1-638-78026-7
R1

RISE & SHINE

DAILY AFFIRMATIONS

for women

Morning Motivation to
Inspire Positivity and Self-Love

JESSICA THIEFELS

**ROCKRIDGE
PRESS**

Introduction

Inspiration and motivation can feel elusive in the morning. You may be tired, already feeling stressed, and perhaps in a rush to get started with your day. What you might not know is that morning magic is already there for you—you just need to take a few minutes to find it. You don't need to roll out a yoga mat at sunrise or create a rigid routine that doesn't flex with your schedule. All you have to do is take five minutes and open this book!

As a coach, entrepreneur, and lover of all things personal development, I've been using affirmations and simple daily exercises for many years. I also regularly share them with my communities and clients, and the value is undeniable. I've discovered that often, all we need is the reminder that we're strong to actually feel that power flowing through us.

This type of work is especially useful in the morning—this well-spent time can dictate what the rest of your day looks like. When you rush through the morning feeling stressed and anxious, you probably notice those same feelings dragging you down all day. On the other hand, when you make a conscious choice to slow down and take time for yourself, even for just five minutes, you can feel a greater sense of ease and purpose that stays with you throughout the day. That's no coincidence. The morning can be a mirror for what comes after.

Here's the thing: I know you have a lot going on, and perhaps your morning routine isn't flexible. That's okay. You don't have to upend your life. All you have to do is learn to use these two powerful tools: affirmations and Rise and Shines.

Affirmations are simple phrases that can be used as an anchor, not just for your morning, but your entire day. They're used to affirm your power, inspiration, and confidence, especially when you're feeling depleted, frustrated, or less than your best. Simply repeat the affirmation, out loud or in your head, to shift back into your power.

All the affirmations shared in this book come from my personal experiences with growth and empowerment. To make the most of each one, you need to focus on truly believing the affirmation as you say it, even if it feels like you're faking it at first. Say each one with meaning and notice how your chest opens and your heart expands. Hold on to that feeling—that's the magic you're looking for!

Rise and Shines are just as powerful. They're short, evidence-based exercises inspired by the practices that have helped me and many of my clients shift into a more positive state. In just a few moments, you'll power up and tap into your confidence through movement, journaling, mindset work, and visualization. These exercises will help you build new habits as they begin shifting your mindset so your confidence and positive energy comes with greater ease each morning.

If you commit to using these tools and taking this small window of time each day, you'll go from feeling stressed, tired, and anxious to confident, empowered, and inspired. All you have to do is grab a cup of your favorite morning elixir and get ready to experience the morning magic that's waiting for you!

I am like the sun. I rise each morning, ready to shine a light on those around me, and set on the horizon each evening, knowing I've done what I came here to do.

*Inspiration comes in the morning,
when I close all the tabs of
yesterday in my mind and let
my brain wander to places
unknown and exciting.*

I am limitless and determined. Nothing can hold me back from getting what I desire when I set the intention to be motivated and purposeful.

When I take care of myself in the morning, I am kinder to myself all day long, no matter what the day brings.

I am powerful beyond measure.
If I want something, it's only a
matter of time before I achieve it.

*Today I will try my best
in everything that I do.
If my best doesn't feel like
enough, I'll remind myself
that by simply trying,
I'm doing enough.*

RISE & SHINE

A SIMPLE WAY TO SHIFT INTO A MORE

empowered state is to understand what you're feeling first thing in the morning. It can be easy to ignore what's bubbling under the surface, like stress and irritation, when you start your day without any reflection.

Grab your journal and write down the three emotions you're feeling right now. Be specific. Are you feeling stressed or anxious? Perhaps you're feeling exhausted or lonely. If you have trouble identifying your feelings, do an internet search for "feelings wheel" to get some ideas, and write down the three feelings that resonate most.

Now, choose the three feelings you'd like to experience instead. Visualize yourself going about your day in this new state. How do you act? What do you say? What choices do you make? Visualizing in the morning is like rehearsing. Use this time to practice how you want to go about your day based on what you want to feel—this way, it's easier to tap into that new way of being all day long.

I allow myself to feel the entire spectrum of feelings, because experiencing sadness is just as important as experiencing happiness— I learn and grow from both.

*I am in charge of my future.
I can change the habits that
no longer serve me and
alter the trajectory of my
life for the better.*

*I am pure magic in a
physical being, and the
morning reminds me that
I can create anything
I want. All I have to do is
see it, feel it, and move
toward it.*

Confidence flows through me, swirling from my head to my fingertips and down to my toes. I choose to tap into that confidence all day long.

I am renewed each morning. The worries of yesterday are behind me, and the possibility of a new day is all I can see ahead.

I am patient with myself as I grow into the next level of who I'm meant to be. I see glimpses of that extraordinary person, and she guides me throughout each day.

RISE & SHINE

FIND INSPIRATION AND CONFIDENCE

this morning by setting an intention. This allows you to clarify what you want to achieve for the day. When you know what you want to happen, you'll know what you're aiming for. Like choosing the route you plan to take, your morning intention makes it easy to navigate your day feeling empowered and inspired.

Journal what you plan to do today and how you want to feel as you do it. For example: *I will finish the project at work with ease. I will talk to my boss about my promotion with confidence. I will finish the day feeling accomplished and give myself the rest I deserve.*

Come back to your intention regularly to make sure you're on course. If you lose your way, remember that things come up and get in the way—that's okay. Every moment is an opportunity to re-center, so take a deep breath and reconnect to your intention.

I am empowered, confident, inspired, and self-assured when I come back to what I know: My value and my worth can only be determined by me.

Even when my path is winding and the destination isn't clear, I navigate every step of the journey with confidence and clarity.

I look at the world through the lens of positivity today, knowing that what I choose to see is what I experience in my life.

*My words matter, and
I choose them with care
and intention to make
everyone around me feel
worthy and valuable.*

Being me is my superpower. Trying to be anyone else dulls my shine and makes it harder for me to give all that I have to give.

Motivation is always available to me. All I have to do is say, "I am ready"—and believe that I am—for it to come quickly and easily.

RISE & SHINE

THIS MORNING, TAP INTO YOUR STRENGTHS

with visualization. Start by writing your top three strengths on a piece of paper. These can be related to your personal life or work, or a mixture of both. Take time creating this list, and choose the strengths that you truly believe you have. It's okay if this is hard. Stick with it until you have all of them.

With your list written, sit back and close your eyes. Take a deep breath and visualize your first strength in action, where you're exhibiting that strength so well, it's undeniable that you're amazing at it. When you feel power and confidence swelling in your body, move to the next strength.

When you finish visualizing all three strengths on your list, you'll stand up stronger than when you sat down. Keep your list of top strengths with you today, and reach for it when you need an extra boost of confidence.

*My experiences remind
me that I've earned the right
to feel empowered, because
I've worked hard to be where
I am today—and no one can
take that away from me.*

I start the day with gratitude so I can see all that I have in every situation, even when things are challenging.

Self-love comes easily to me when I remember that I am human and that making mistakes or struggling to keep up only means I am making an effort.

*I look forward to tackling
any challenge that comes
my way today, because
I know I can handle
it with wisdom, grace,
and confidence.*

Creative ideas are always within me, and I can access them easily when I let my mind run freely and without judgment.

*I am open to every
opportunity that comes my
way today, because I shed
the worries of yesterday
and step into the power
that's waiting for me today.*

RISE & SHINE

THE GOAL OF THIS RISE AND SHINE IS

to connect with your body and let any worries or stress roll off your shoulders. The practice is simple: walk around your house or your neighborhood for at least five minutes. As you start walking, take three deep breaths, in and out.

While you walk, notice the feeling in your feet as they make contact with the ground. Notice how your knees bend and the feeling of your pants on your legs. Notice your hands and arms. What are they doing? Are they swinging? Touching your sides?

If you prefer, instead of walking, you can move in any way that is comfortable for you. The important part is to be mindful of how your body is moving and feeling at the present moment.

When you get into your body like this, feeling all the different sensations while you walk, it's hard to be in your head, where stress and worry live. Use this as an opportunity to clear space in your mind for a fresh and inspired new day.

I am filled with hope and excitement for all that's ahead of me, because I know that each step I take is bringing me closer to the vision I have for myself.

*When I believe in myself,
I set the tone for how others
see me, what they say to
me, and how I react to their
opinions and feedback.*

I know that everything is happening when it should and as it should and that all I desire is making its way to me.

*I love who I'm becoming
and the experiences that
have brought me here. If
it weren't for what's behind
me, I wouldn't be able to
reach what's ahead.*

It's normal to feel
frustrated or angry, but
I can determine the mindset
and actions that I bring
to the rest of my day,
regardless of my emotions.

*When I start the day by
connecting with myself,
I tap into an infinite source
of creativity within me.*

RISE & SHINE

EAT A BREAKFAST THAT MAKES YOU FEEL GOOD

this morning. It can be easy to grab something unhealthy on the go or forgo breakfast altogether, but this leaves you feeling depleted throughout the day, as well as more stressed, less productive, and quicker to react negatively.

Today, power up your morning by making something at home that's nutritious and filled with protein, healthy fats, and some carbohydrates—but don't stop there. Eat it sitting down, away from distractions like your email or phone. Take each bite with intention, noticing how it tastes and how good it feels to take care of your body.

This is mindful eating, a simple practice that helps you feel more satiated and fulfilled with your meal so you don't overeat or miss the meal altogether! When finished, take care of your dishes so you don't have to stress about doing them later.

I feel more powerful than my self-doubt, because its presence reminds me that I am pushing myself to my limits—and that's a good thing.

*I choose to put the
challenges and obstacles
of yesterday behind me
and step into this new day
with a fresh outlook on
what's possible.*

I forgive myself for what went wrong in the past, because I know that I am always doing my best with the tools that I have at any given moment.

I love all the aspects of my personality that make me who I am. Without them, I wouldn't be able to bring my own unique magic to the world.

I choose to take feedback from others only when it serves my highest good, not when it makes me believe I am less than or not enough.

I accept myself today,
tomorrow, and every day
as a brilliant yet flawed
human being who is
simply doing my best to
love, nurture, and care for
myself and others.

RISE & SHINE

LISTEN TO THE WORDS YOU USE

when speaking to yourself today. Our inner dialogue has a significant impact on how we feel and what we accomplish. Think about it: If you consistently tell yourself that what you're doing is not enough, you're more stressed and anxious, constantly trying to do more, running on a hamster wheel of your own making.

We believe what we tell ourselves over and over. If, instead, you consistently tell yourself that you're doing your best, you'll start to believe it. If we're going to tell ourselves anything, why wouldn't we choose to tell ourselves something positive and loving?

Think of it as speaking to yourself the way you would to your best friend. Test yourself throughout the day: If you wouldn't say it to your best friend, resist the urge to say it to yourself. Instead, rewrite the thought to be more positive and uplifting.

I am worthy of love simply because I exist. There is nothing I need to do to earn the love and respect of those around me.

*I am drawn to people who
lift me up and help me live
with purpose, and I choose to
walk away from those who
bring me down.*

Confidence radiates from me today, as I walk with my head high, my heart open, and my feet firmly rooted in the ground.

When I take time to honor and care for myself each morning, I am able to be a role model for the power of self-love.

I am my greatest advocate, and I ask for what I need, even when my voice is shaking and I'm unsure of what the outcome will be.

I am inspired to improve my little corner of the world today. I don't need to change the world to have an impact on the people around me.

RISE & SHINE

LOOK IN THE MIRROR THIS MORNING

and say three things that you love about yourself. These can be related to your physical appearance, your personality, something you've accomplished—anything that you truly love about who you are. You might say:

- I love the color of my eyes.
- I love that I did a great job on that project yesterday.
- I love the perfectly imperfect waves of my hair in the morning.

Finish by looking into your own eyes and saying: *I love you.* But don't just do this in the morning. Do it every time you look in the mirror throughout the day. This may sound cheesy, and it can be hard at first, but this consistent practice is a way of rewiring the pathways in your brain. Over time, you'll train your brain to automatically find the positive aspects that you love about yourself, making your self-talk more uplifting in the process.

Gratitude is like a warm jacket I choose to put on every single morning. When I wear it, I feel comforted and calm, ready to share the warmth with those around me.

Today I choose to take the
first step toward what
I want, because even small
steps propel me forward
toward the life I am
choosing to create.

Self-love makes me power-ful, because it reminds me that all I need to do is give myself encouragement to remember how valued and worthy I am.

I speak to myself with love and kindness, no matter how frustrated or stressed I am, because lifting myself up helps me do my best all day long.

I am full of untapped potential, and by simply choosing to achieve something, I set in motion the wheels of success—all I have to do is keep them moving.

I am alive, and today that is enough. I do not need to accomplish anything noteworthy to end the day feeling as though I have been successful.

RISE & SHINE

STRETCH YOUR BODY TO RELEASE ANY

tension you woke up with today. You don't need to roll out a yoga mat; instead, just move your body in a way that feels relieving and nurturing. Here are a few simple stretches you can try:

- Stand tall, feet shoulder-width apart, and reach your hands above your head. Stretch your body from side to side, holding each side for as long as it feels good.
- Sit on the floor with your legs stretched out in front of you and reach toward your toes. You'll feel an elongating stretch in your spine.
- Stand with your feet shoulder-width apart and arms out to the side, palms facing forward. Gently push your chest out, raise your face to the sky, roll your shoulders back, and feel your heart open.

Take deep breaths as you enjoy each stretch, letting the worries of yesterday dissipate with each movement.

Inspiration comes easily to me this morning, because I know that it's already inside me and all I have to do is let it flow through me.

Today I see the world through the eyes of a child. I choose fun and excitement and put my worries and stresses aside, if only for one day.

I am grateful for all that I have, even when it feels like it's not enough, because simply feeling gratitude allows me to see the abundance that's all around me.

I continue moving toward what I want, even if my legs are shaking, because I am certain that I can attain the life I see for myself.

I decide what my day looks like instead of letting the day decide for me. All I have to do is choose, and life begins to shift in my direction.

I tap into my authenticity so it's easy for me to see what I truly want and what I no longer need, intentionally creating a life I love.

RISE & SHINE

TAKE JUST FIVE MINUTES TO BE STILL THIS MORNING.

This is the same as meditation, but don't get caught up in the label of "meditation" and what you "should" do. Instead, find a quiet place and follow these simple steps:

1. Set an alarm for five minutes.
2. Sit or stand comfortably and gently close your eyes.
3. Let your shoulders and body relax.
4. Take slow, deep breaths, in and out, counting to three as you inhale and five as you exhale.
5. If thoughts arise, let them float away like a cloud or a balloon and come back to counting your breaths.
6. When your alarm goes off, start your day feeling relaxed and calm.

This practice is a simple way to center yourself in the morning. Instead of getting lost in your to-do list, stillness gives you a chance to slow down, which sets the tone for your entire day.

I am the creator of my day, and this morning I get to choose what I will feel, do, and be when I walk out the front door.

*I am confident in what
I have to offer in every area
of my life, and I will bring
that powerful mindset to
everything I do today.*

My creativity and inspiration are easy to access when I practice self-love, because they allow me to embrace all that I have to offer.

*I take active steps toward
what I want and trust
that I'm on the right path,
knowing that the rest is
falling into place.*

I let go of fear, open my heart, and stand taller, knowing that I can handle whatever comes my way today.

*I give my full attention
to everyone I speak with
today, because this allows
me to connect more deeply
and opens me up to new
opportunities.*

RISE & SHINE

TAKE FIVE MINUTES THIS MORNING TO RELAX

with a calming body scan. Simply relax each body part as you think of it, moving from your toes to the top of your head and back down. Stay at each body part for a few seconds before moving to the next.

1. Sit comfortably and close your eyes.
2. Take three deep breaths. When you feel relaxed, start your body scan, focusing first on the front of your body.
3. Call to mind your toes and feel them relax. Move next to the tops of your feet, shins, quadriceps, stomach, chest, shoulders, ears, face, and top of your head.
4. Move to the back of your body, starting with the back of your head, then your upper back, lower back, hips, hamstrings, calves, heels, and bottoms of your feet.
5. Feel the relaxation flow throughout your body, and carry that with you all day long.

I step fully into my power today, embracing my strengths and knowing that by simply bringing my gifts to the world, I'm living out my purpose.

The more I give others the space to live powerfully and authentically, the easier it is for me to create the same space for myself.

Today I set a single intention: to see myself through the eyes of someone who truly loves me. When I do this, self-love comes easily and effortlessly.

*I take a deep breath
and am renewed by the
rays of the morning's sun,
as they wash away the
worries and stresses of
yesterday, allowing me to
start fresh today.*

I close my eyes, breathe in deep, and allow the limitless potential of a new day to fill my body with hope, confidence, and a renewed sense of energy.

*I let go of what no longer
serves me, because I trust
that what I need and want
will come to me when I
release anything that's
holding me back.*

RISE & SHINE

START YOUR DAY BY WRITING A "TO-BE" LIST.

We can be so focused on what we need to *do* that we forget about who we want to *be* each day. It's easier to get caught up in the stress or chaos of the day when we're only focused on getting things done, rather than putting the focus on feeling or being a certain way. As a result, we let the day decide how we act and feel rather than deciding for ourselves.

For example, your to-be list might include: calm, positive, happy, and energetic. By getting clear on this before you start the day, you get to choose how you will be throughout the day, no matter what comes your way. If you get frustrated or run into a challenge, you can come back to your to-be list to remember how you want to be at that moment.

I embrace my most authentic self, because that's what will bring me closer and closer to the goals I've set for myself and get me across the finish line.

*I keep my eyes and mind
wide open so I can spot
every opportunity that
presents itself to me today,
no matter how big or small.*

*I release the beliefs that
tell me I am not inspired,
courageous, or powerful
enough, so I can truly share
my whole self with the world.*

I learn to love myself with each day that I release criticism and open myself to my kindness.

I am inspired when I allow myself to simply be, instead of trying to change who I am to fit the needs of others.

*The people who love me
are ready to help and
encourage me whenever
I need it and ask for it.*

RISE & SHINE

TAKE TIME THIS MORNING TO SEE THE

abundance all around you. It's easy to live life in a mindset of wishing for what you don't have or what you think you need. Shifting into a mindset of abundance fills you with a sense of fulfillment and gratitude for all you have rather than stress or anxiety about what you don't.

Make a list in your journal or simply say it to yourself. Your list might include:

- I am abundant in clothing, with a closet full of clothes that keep me warm.
- I am abundant in opportunities to learn, because every challenge teaches me something.
- I am abundant in water, with a tap that I can drink from whenever I need.

Bring this mindset of abundance to everything you do today, reminding yourself how abundant you are, no matter what the circumstances.

I keep all judgments to myself throughout the day and give everyone around me the space they need to be their own unique self.

*I choose to take on my
responsibilities with a
smile, because it's in the
doing that I find inspiration
is already within me.*

*Today I let go of right
and wrong and embrace
the power of compromise
to find compassion and
stress-free solutions when
issues arise.*

*Today I choose to love myself
the way my best friends
love me—without judgment,
question, or agenda, even
when I don't think
I deserve it.*

*When I live as my most
authentic self and tap
into the unique gifts only
I possess, I'm able to gain
momentum and create
change in my life.*

I transform negative messages into empowering ones. When I do this, my self-talk changes from "I can't do that" to "I am learning . . ."

RISE & SHINE

PUT ON YOUR FAVORITE SONG AND DANCE

this morning. Or just move your body without the music, if you prefer. Our bodies are made up of energy, and when we move, we allow stagnant energy to shift. Think of your body like that candy bar stuck in the vending machine. With a little movement, you can shake it out.

With that stagnant energy shaken out, you may notice you feel lighter or more expansive throughout your entire day. This is because dancing reduces stress, increases blood flow, boosts your mood, and stimulates positive memories. To reap all these benefits, all you have to do is put on your favorite tune, close your eyes, and move like no one is watching.

Use this same practice anytime you need a pick-me-up. Turn on your favorite song when you're going to the store or after dealing with a challenging issue and dance it out.

I listen attentively, actively, and with compassion, because when I do, the people around me feel heard and understood.

I accept myself fully and unconditionally, releasing feelings of criticism and judgment, and instead choose love and kindness.

*Today I get to tackle
everything on my to-do list.
I don't have to or need to;
I am choosing to, because
my future self will thank me.*

I allow myself to lean on my community when I am struggling, stressed, or uncertain, because they support me lovingly and without judgment.

*If I don't ask for what
I want, the answer is always
no, so I speak up about what
I need and welcome the
kindness I receive.*

I can see all my untapped potential when I close my eyes and visualize my future self taking risks and trusting the process.

RISE & SHINE

TAKE TIME TO SPRUCE UP YOUR HOME

this morning, from the bedroom to the kitchen. A cluttered physical space leads to a cluttered mind, which makes it harder to tap into your confidence and motivation throughout the day. This doesn't mean you need to pull out the mop and run the vacuum. Instead, focus on small cleaning opportunities that will help your morning feel more put together, like:

- Making the bed
- Washing the dishes
- Clearing the countertop
- Organizing the bathroom
- Putting clean clothes away

These seemingly small tasks can make all the difference in how you approach your day. With a fresh space, you can tap into a fresh mindset. Look around, take a deep breath, and get ready to bring a clear head to everything you do today.

I am grateful for my friendships, because they anchor me in stormy weather, allow me to blossom in the sun, and lift my soul when I'm feeling low.

I choose to see myself through the eyes of my biggest fan today, so no matter what I do or don't do, I am reminded to love myself completely and without question.

When I get curious about the people around me, rather than being critical, I am able to see the kind of person I do and don't wish to become.

I am intentional about my choices and bring clarity to every decision I make today, so I can create the life I want to live.

I see compromise as an opportunity to practice compassion for others, which in turn reminds me to have the same understanding for myself.

*I feel the magic bubbling
under my skin and rising to
the surface, and I let it spill
out of me and into the world.*

RISE & SHINE

LET THE WORLD INSPIRE YOU THIS MORNING.

It can be hard to tap into inspiration when you're focused on what's happening in your immediate world. Broaden your lens and find the inspiration inside you with this simple practice. Grab your favorite morning beverage, find a window where you can sit or stand comfortably, and get curious about what you see outside.

For just five minutes, open your eyes to everything that's happening, like the wind blowing, a bird chirping, or someone walking by. Get out of your head and let yourself be curious. This time will provide you with a few moments of stillness; even better, it'll remind you of the inspiration that is all around if you stop to see it.

The person walking with a hop in their step may be the encouragement you need to shift your mood. The birds chirping may be a reminder that life can be simple and carefree.

I let go of black-and-white thinking today, because my goal is not to be right, but to be inclusive of others' perspectives.

I am empowered by my to-do list, because it reminds me that I am playing an active role in my own life, creating and building with each new day.

I am the director of my life.
I prepare the scene, choose
the actors, and turn my life
into an award-winning film
that I'm proud to call mine.

My courage is easily accessible at any given moment, and I can call on it to help me feel empowered and determined, no matter the situation.

*Today I choose to smile
through the challenges,
see opportunity in the
setbacks, and welcome the
fear, because nothing and
no one can slow me down.*

I release any stress and anxiety from yesterday and allow the promise of a new day to bring me ease and optimism.

RISE & SHINE

TAKE TIME THIS MORNING TO FORGIVE

yourself. If you're holding on to and continually punishing yourself for old mistakes, you may find it more difficult to love who you are today. Luckily, you can start tapping into your self-compassion by forgiving yourself.

Grab your journal and start a list, with a goal of forgiving yourself for at least three things. Start each item on the list with, "I forgive myself for . . ." Repeat each one out loud or in your head. Say it with compassion, as if you're speaking to a dear friend.

This can be an emotional practice, so let tears flow or feelings rise to the surface; this is an important part of the release. Forgiveness might not come right away, and that's okay. Allowing yourself to look at repressed feelings is a powerful practice that will lead to a sense of lightness and self-love.

Today I choose to make healthy food choices, because nourishing my body is a simple act of self-love that I can choose multiple times a day.

I listen to my loved ones without expectation or agenda so they're able to share freely and openly—this creates a space of compassion and love.

I am confident in who
I am, knowing that
negative comments from
others are simply a
reflection of their
insecurities, not my worth
or value in this world.

I surround myself with people who love powerfully, give completely, and hold space for me, and I am inspired to do the same for them.

I easily and confidently walk away from people who treat me poorly, because they're not worth my time or energy.

Today I bring joy to everything I do, regardless of what's going on around me, because I am the only person responsible for my happiness.

RISE & SHINE

THIS MORNING, FIND THE TIME AND SPACE

to be with yourself without any distractions. Think about how your body and mind change the very moment you look at your email and social media. Your shoulders tense up, your body tightens, and you may feel a sense of dread. There's so much to do and so many expectations.

Instead, give yourself time to gently shift from sleep into waking:

- Take a mindful shower, feeling the water washing over your skin and smelling the soap. Turn all your senses on and tune in to the present moment.
- In your mind or journal, list three people you're grateful for and why you're grateful for them. If possible, call or send them a message today thanking them for being in your life. Gratitude helps release toxic emotions and supports stress regulation.

Memorize that sense of calm in your body, and come back to it as needed throughout your day.

*I can easily find calm,
even in the roughest
storms, because that
sense of peace is already
within me.*

*I listen to my own
needs and tend to them
as I would a friend's
needs—with understanding,
love, and attentiveness.*

*I am excited to connect
with people who lift me
up and support me on
this journey of creating
a better life for myself.*

I take deep breaths this morning to tap into a sense of calm, and I continually come back to this practice when I need it.

*I set a clear intention
in the morning so I know
what I need to do to
feel my best throughout
the day.*

*I forgive myself for
any mistakes I made
yesterday and shift back
into my power today.*

RISE & SHINE

ENVISION THE MOST INSPIRED,

confident, and empowered version of yourself. This person is inside you, but if you don't know what she's like or how she acts, how can you ever be her? So take a moment to consider her.

Start by writing down the top 10 characteristics of this person. Is she charismatic? Determined? Empowered? Next, envision what she acts like and how she carries herself. Be specific and have fun with it.

Finally, recall a recent moment when you felt less than confident, and imagine what she would have done and said. For example, she may have asked for the raise that you were too nervous to bring up in your annual review.

Now, your job is to be her. Next time you're in a situation where you're not feeling empowered, ask yourself: What would she do? Choose as if you are her—because you are!

*I am so in love with
the progress I'm making,
every time I look in the
mirror, I say to myself,
"You're incredible!"*

I love all the new pieces of me that are wriggling into place, and I let go of the ones that are slowly falling away to make space for who I am becoming.

My personal power is restored with each deep breath I take today. All I need is 30 seconds of calm to feel confident and in control.

*I am guided by my fear,
because I know that when
I'm scared, I'm stepping
outside my comfort zone,
and that's a powerful
place to be.*

*I connect to my desires
and dreams when I start
my day, so I can step into
who I want to be and what
I want to achieve.*

I remember to continually believe in myself throughout the day by lovingly repeating the phrase "I believe in you" whenever I feel doubt or uncertainty.

RISE & SHINE

GET INTO THE MINDSET OF SUCCESS

this morning. The goal of this practice is to remind yourself of all your accomplishments. Grab your journal, find a comfortable place to write, and start a list of your achievements from every area of your life, including:

- Personal
- Family
- Work
- Volunteer
- Health
- Hobbies

It can be easy to focus on the one or two things we're struggling with, but success is actually all around us. For example, planning your first-ever family trip is just as much of an accomplishment as getting the job you want. When you take time to create this list, you'll see that you're successful in many areas of your life.

Use this list to propel yourself forward today, whether you're struggling to get something done or questioning if you're good enough. You can step into the mindset of success simply by remembering all that you've accomplished thus far.

My capacity for fearless self-acceptance is limitless, because it requires no validation or approval from anyone or anything outside myself.

*I am in awe of all that
I've accomplished in my
life, even the things that
seemed small at the time.*

What I say to myself matters, so I am delicate and intentional with the words I choose, ensuring they always come from a place of love, kindness, and confidence.

The right people and opportunities find me when I choose to flow instead of force.

*I lean into my inner
source of self-compassion
throughout the day,
even when I'd rather
fight against it.*

*I am patient with myself
as I grow and learn,
because becoming who
I want to be is a lifelong
journey, and I'm enjoying
the ride.*

About the Author

Jessica Thiefels is a published author, host of the podcast *Mindset Reset Radio*, and CEO of Jessica Thiefels Consulting. She's been writing for more than 10 years and has been featured in top publications including *Forbes* and *Entrepreneur*. After traveling the world for eight months in 2019, Jessica came back with a mission to empower women to make their own rules and live with intention, so they can wake up every day excited about the extraordinary life they get to live.

CPSIA information can be obtained
at www.ICGtesting.com
Printed in the USA
BVHW050242180122
626412BV00001B/1

9 781638 073673